Mystie's Activities for

Bereaved Children

Grades K-2

Utilizing
<u>For the Love of Emrys</u>

KIDS' GRIEF RELIEF

Hi, I'm Mystie. What's *Dragon - You - Down?*

www.KidsGriefRelief.org

A 501(c)(3) NonProfit

Grief Support to Empower Bereaved Children

ISBN: 978-0-9856334-7-9

(softcover book)

My Special Activity Booklet about
_____ and me.

Activity 1A

MY FAMILY MEMBERS

Circle the ones you live with

My special person who died: _____

Hi Kids!
My name is Mystie. I'm a mystical, magical dragonfly from a far away planet.

What's your name?

What grade are you in?

How old are you?

Who died?

Share your cover picture with your group.

Are you feeling dragged—down because someone you love has died?

I felt dragged—down when my best friend suddenly died. I knew I would never see him again. It felt awful. I couldn't even fly.

I was feeling

GRIEF.

When I first flew to Earth, I thought Earth dragonflies lived forever like the dragonflies on Nilrem, where I come from.

So when I met Darvy, the Earth dragonfly, I thought we would be friends for a long time. But I was wrong. Earth dragonflies have a short life.

Darvy and I had so much fun together! We flew wildly all over the marsh at the edge of the beach, where we lived. We laughed and played all day long. I loved being with him!

Then one day while we were playing dragonfly tag, he died. He suddenly stopped flying and fell to the ground. I was shocked. I felt terrible. I couldn't believe what happened.

We had a funeral, and buried him near a special rock where we used to sit and talk. I cried and cried.

I had a lot of different feelings. Some of the feelings are listed on the next page. What are YOU feeling?

Activity 3B

How are you feeling?

What are you thinking about? Do you know why you feel this way?
What do you wish would happen?

Good or Great
Positive or excellent ...
no problems or worries!

OK
Acceptable but not great ...
something seems out of place.

Friendly
Wanting to spend time with
others or getting to know new
people.

Loving
Wanting to hug or share
because of a special connection
or friendship.

Energetic
Lots of activity and physical
expression coming from inside
you that must come out!

Hopeful
Wishing for ... looking forward
to ... or expecting something.

Stressed
Upset by what is happening and
uncertain about the future.

Mad
Upset about something ...
things are not going the way
you want them to.

Confused
Can't think clearly, and not sure
what's happening.

Lonely
Needing a friend or a hug ...
being apart from others.

Sad
Not happy because something
bad has happened to you or
someone you know.

Shocked
Surprised, but not in a good way.

Feeling Something Else
You know how you feel, but it's
not included on this chart.

Draw Your Emotion/Face Here::

Feelings Keep Changing
You know how you feel, but it
changes a lot. Or you're
feeling a lot of different ways
all at the same time.

What would you call this emotion/face?

Activity 4

When I was feeling dragged—down about Darvy's death, the beautiful colors in my wings were all muddied up. I had so many feelings.

----------What colors show your feelings?------------

For example, what color shows you're sad? Blue? Gray?

What color shows you're upset? You're worried?

Would you color in my wings to show how you feel?

When you're GRIEVING, you might have pains in your body, like a stomach ache or headache. You might feel extra tired.

How does your body feel?

Color in the parts of your body that feel different since the death of your loved one.

In the circle below, write down the names of all the children in your grief group, including yourself.

If you agree to keep confidential what is spoken in your group, trace over the dashes.

Activity 7

Hi Kids! How are you feeling today?

Let's start today by practicing Compassion.

Compassion comes from a loving heart.
You can speak words of Compassion to other children in your group. Having someone care helps a person who is feeling grief.

Here are some ideas of what to say:
As you listen and read the words, choose one to say to someone else in the group.

"Your _____ loved you a lot. I know you're going to miss her. I bet you have lots of great memories about her.

"I'm sorry to hear about the death of _____. You must miss him very much."

"I know you feel really sad about _____ dying. It's okay to feel sad and upset about it."

Activity 8

Everyone grieves differently.

There's no right or wrong way.

You're grieving the way you need to.

It's okay to feel mad, sad or upset.

It's okay to cry.

I grieved for many months.

Remember I told you how my beautiful wings were way dragged-down and muddied up when my friend died?

Eventually I felt better. My friend Lark, the dolphin, helped me alot. She listened to me and helped me understand that what I was feeling was normal.

Now I really LOVE to help children like you feel better!

Activity 9A

In the heart below, write down
the names of the people and pets,
who are helping you feel better.

Do you know what a memory is?

In the box below, draw a picture of your favorite memory with your loved one.

My Favorite Memory

1	2	3	4	5
What is the first and last name of your special person?	Did your special person teach you anything?	Do you know your special person's birthday? (Day/Month/Year)	Was your special person buried or cremated?	Did your special person like to wear jewelry? What kind?
6	**7**	**8**	**9**	**10**
Describe a special holiday spent with your special person.	Tell about the last time you saw your special person.	What name did your special person call you?	Tell about a funny moment with your special person.	Describe a trip you took with your special person.
11	**12**	**13**	**14**	**15**
Tell about what kind of clothes your special person liked to wear.	Tell about an object that reminds you of your special person.	What kind of music did your special person enjoy?	What kind of movies did your special person like to watch?	Did your special person ever have a pet?
16	**17**	**18**	**19**	**20**
Did your special person have a favorite saying - what was it?	Tell about a sad memory with your favorite person.	Tell about some of the people who loved your special person.	What one thing always makes you think about your special person?	What's your favorite photo of your special person? Describe it.
21	**22**	**23**	**24**	**25**
Tell about something your special person loved to do.	What time of day do you feel "dragged-down" over the death of your special person?	What's the one thing you will miss MOST about your special person?	Do you feel peaceful about the way your special person was buried? Why?	Tell about a gift you gave your special person.

Activity 11

What special things do you have to remind yourself about your loved one who died? Make a list.

Where do you keep your special things?

Activity 12

Hi Kids! How are you feeling today?

Look at the mobile of me. Can you bend my wings to show everyone how you've been feeling the past week?

When you're grieving over someone, parts of you may be happy, yet parts still may be sad or upset.

Use my four wings to show your feelings.

Activity 13

Did you read about my friend Christina? I helped her when her dog died. She was really sad.

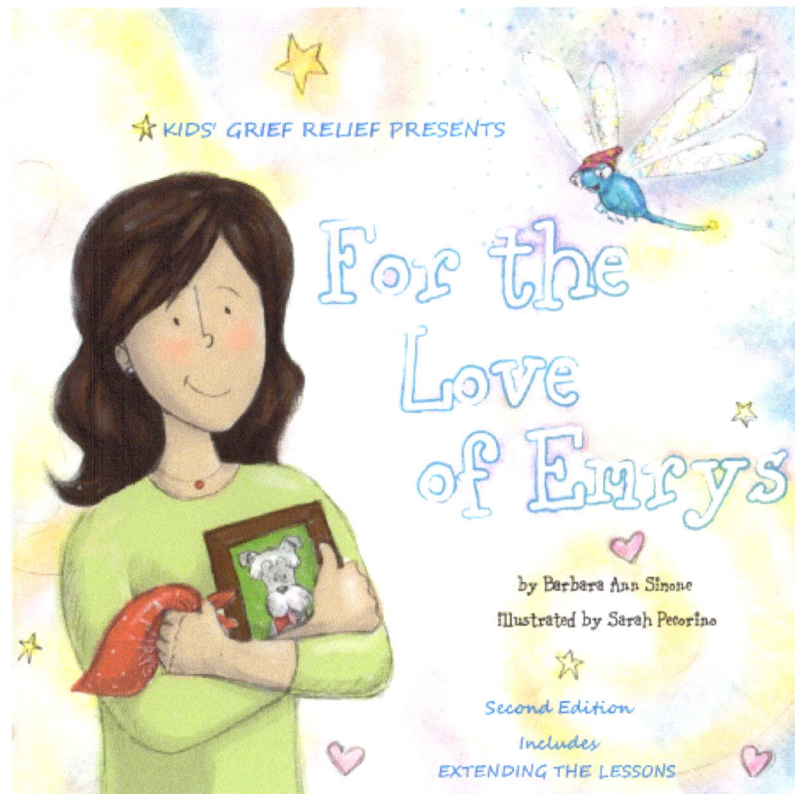

☆ KIDS' GRIEF RELIEF PRESENTS

For the Love of Emrys

by Barbara Ann Sinone

Illustrated by Sarah Pecorino

☆

Second Edition

Includes
EXTENDING THE LESSONS

At the end of her story, Christina feels a lot better. She knows Emrys will always be in her heart. She has lots of love to share with others; she'll love them for the rest of her life.

BEFORE Emrys died we played together every day.

He listened to me and sat on my lap all the time.

I loved to pet him and take care of him. My favorite time of the day was when we ran together. He was fast!

Tell about times BEFORE your loved one died.

I was with Emrys THE DAY HE DIED. He became very sick. His body stopped working.

I took his body to the vet. I was upset and sad.

It was hard to come home and see all his playthings. I wanted so much for him to be alive, but he wasn't.

Tell about THE DAY YOUR LOVED ONE DIED.

AFTER EMRYS DIED, I felt very alone. No one will ever take his place in my heart.

I think about him a lot. I am happy that we had so much fun when he was alive.

As I grow up, I want to always remember how he loved me and how I loved him.

Tell about AFTER YOUR LOVED ONE DIED.

Activity 16B

Christina believed Emrys' spirit was in heaven after he died.

Where do you believe your special person's spirit is?

Draw a picture of what it looks like.

Activity 18

Through her grief, Christina learned that the love in her heart is changeless. She will always love Emrys. She loved him when he was alive, and continues to love him even though he is gone.

Your love for your special person will be inside your heart forever, too.

Look at the heart below.

On the left side of the heart, write about how you showed love for your special person before he/she died.

On the right side write or draw pictures of how you show you still love him/her.

Loving yourself, by doing things you enjoy can help you move through grief.

Think about ways you can help yourself to feel better. You can draw pictures or write down your ideas.

When I feel sad I can

When I feel worried I can

When I feel scared I can

When I feel angry I can

When I feel upset I can

When I feel _____ I can

What's your favorite thing to do?
Close your eyes for a moment,
and pretend you are doing it.

Now, color and decorate my wings to show how
you feel when you're doing your favorite thing.

I know you can't fly
like me, but you can
feel like you're flying,
when you're doing
something you
really enjoy.

Activity 20B

©2014 Kids' Grief Relief

Here's another way to help yourself when you're feeling dragged—down.

It's all about BREATHING.

When you take the time to control how you breathe, you can help yourself handle some of the dragged—down emotions of grief.

You will feel more relaxed and calm. Your body gets the air it needs to calm itself down.

That feels good.

breeeathe

What do you like to think about?

Your thoughts can make you feel dragged-down, really happy, or somewhere in between.

Here are some "Dragged—Down" thoughts you might be thinking. Are any of these familiar to you? If so, trace over the arrow with your marker or crayon.

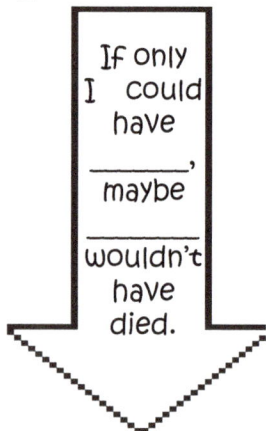

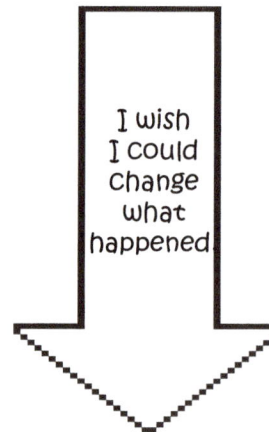

IT'S

NOT

FAIR!

I should have been nicer to _____.

It's terrible that I will never see _____ again.

If only I could have _____, maybe _____ wouldn't have died.

I wish I could change what happened

Let's throw away all YOUR "Dragged—Down" thoughts.

Activity 23

Now it's time for dragon—fly thoughts! When you think a dragon—fly thought, you feel good inside. Then everything feels better on the outside.

Can you say these aloud?

1. I am brave.

2. I am smart enough to understand what happened.

3. It feels good to talk to others about what happened.

4. I have my own personal feelings about death.

5. I have special memories of _____ that I will always treasure.

6. I like who I am.

7. I am grateful for all the people who love me.

8. I am a powerful kid!

Activity 24

THE BEST thoughts come from your heart.
Think about people, places, pets, and things
you LOVE.

In the hearts below, write down the
names of who and what you LOVE.
Don't forget to include yourself!

Activity 25

Write four dragon—fly thoughts about YOU in the frame.

Draw your picture in the middle.

I am

I am

I am

I am

Activity 26

You've done a great job learning how to deal with the death of your loved one. You are very brave!

Here are some statements about grief.
If you agree with the statement, draw one heart next to it.
If you really, really agree with it, draw two hearts next to it.
If you do not agree, draw an X next to it.

1. It's okay to cry when you feel sad.

2. It's normal to be upset and worried when someone you love has died.

3. Everyone grieves the same way.

4. I know it's okay to tell someone that I don't feel well because I am grieving.

5. I will miss _____ for a long time.

6. I can be happy again, even though _____ had died.

7. Hiding my feelings is a good way to feel better.

8. My positive thoughts help me feel better.

9. Hurting myself or others in school or at home is a good way to express grief.

10. Taking time to breath and relax helps me when I feel upset.

Dear _____

_____
_____
_____
_____
_____
_____
_____
_____
_____
_____
_____

Love Always,

_____

Activity 28

FOREVER CALENDAR

During each and every day,
We Love them.

During each and every night,
We Love them.

During each and every week,
We Love them.

During each and every month,
We Love them.

During each and every season,
We Love them.

During each and every year,
We Love them.

As the days turn into weeks, turn into months,
turn into seasons, turn into years,
We Love them;
Forever.

Activity 29

Bye Kids! I'm leaving you these powerful Heart—Words to say anytime you're feeling some grief.

The Power of my heart is strong
It gently guides me all day long.
If I feel sad throughout the day
This Love reminds me, **I'm still okay!**

Even though my life has changed
Since _____ has gone away,
There is one thing that's always there
It's Love inside my heart to share.

I AM A POWERFUL KID !

Activity 31

www.ingramcontent.com/pod-product-compliance
Lightning Source LLC
LaVergne TN
LVHW072109070426
835509LV00002B/86